99

THOUGHTS

ON

JESUS-CENTERED LIVING

EVERYDAY WAYS
TO WALK WITH
THE REBEL JESUS

RICK LAWRENCE

99 Thoughts on Jesus-Centered Living
Everyday Ways to Walk With the Rebel Jesus

Credits
Author: Rick Lawrence
Executive Developer: Nadim Najm
Chief Creative Officer: Joani Schultz
Copy Editor: Rob Cunningham
Cover Art and Production: Riley Hall
Production Manager: DeAnne Lear

ISBN 978-0-7644-8454-4

10 9 8 7 6 5   20 19 18 17 16 15 14

Printed in the United States of America.

DEDICATION

To Greg Stier of Dare 2 Share, who first introduced
me to the "beeline" of C.H. Spurgeon.

CONTENTS

INTRODUCTION

The planets in our solar system all orbit around the sun, because they have no choice but to orbit around the sun. We, on the other hand, have been given the freedom to choose our own orbits, so to speak. And even though the "planet" I call "me" will sooner or later spin out of control or disintegrate or turn into a flaming ball if I choose to leave the orbit I was created to follow—with Jesus at the center of my life—I have nevertheless chosen to do *just that* during seasons of my life. But two quotes from two great men, separated by a century, sum up the gravitational pull that has drawn me back into my close orbit of the Son, repeatedly and permanently.

In his book *Following Jesus*, the great British theologian N.T. Wright says this: "The longer you look at Jesus, the more you will want to serve him. That is, of course, if it's the real Jesus you're looking at."[1] Wright is saying that it's very possible for us to miss the "real" Jesus—the Jesus described by the Bible who is wholly unlike any man who ever lived because he is both man and God. Instead, many of us end up following a guy who *looks* a lot like Jesus but is actually more like the guy who made your sub sandwich the other day: polite, eager to serve, helpful, and comfortably anonymous. The real Jesus is magnetic, because he is far more fierce, unpredictable, and amazing than our conventionally preposterous descriptions of him.

The second quote is from Charles Haddon Spurgeon, a 19th-century English pastor who suffered from depression and a painful birth defect.

Every week, this 22-year-old phenomenon preached two services at his London church, bellowing his love for the "orbited Son" (without the benefit of a microphone) twice every Sunday to crowds of 6,000 people. At the time, he had more books in print than any other living person. He still has more books in print than any other pastor in history, including more than 2,500 of his published sermons. Historians call him the "Prince of Preachers," and his guiding motto in life has now become my own: "In everything, make a beeline to Jesus." Rather than explain what this little motto means, I'll let this well-known story about Spurgeon do the talking:

> Much later in Spurgeon's ministry, a young pastor asked him to listen to him preach and give him a critique—a common request since Spurgeon was revered by other preachers. After he listened to the young man's impassioned sermon, Spurgeon was honest—he thought it was well prepared and well delivered but it nevertheless…stunk.
>
> "Will you tell me why you think it a poor sermon?" asked the young pastor.
>
> "Because," said Spurgeon, "There was no Christ in it."
>
> The young man said, "Well, Christ was not in the text; we are not to be preaching Christ always, we must preach what is in the text."

The old man responded, "Don't you know, young man, that from every town, and every village, and every little hamlet in England, wherever it may be, there is a road to London?"

"Yes," said the young man.

"Ah!" said the old preacher, "and so from every text in Scripture there is a road to the metropolis of the Scriptures, that is Christ. Dear brother, when you get to a text, say, 'Now, what is the road to Christ?' and then preach a sermon, running along the road towards the great metropolis—Christ."[2]

Spurgeon lived his life "making a beeline to Christ"—it was his central, guiding commitment every time he opened his mouth to speak or teach or write. And as I have adopted "beelining" as the driving force in my life, I have discovered my own embedded purpose and identity—it feels *deeply good* to follow the orbit I was designed by God to follow. And when everything in our life is orbiting around "the real Jesus," epic stuff happens. Because Jesus is at the center of our lives, the people around us find rescue from pain and worry and hopelessness and emptiness and loneliness and purposelessness and so many other "ness-es." Life transcends our expected drudgeries and becomes a grand, breathless adventure.

I've been editor of Group Magazine, the world's most-read resource for Christian youth pastors, for almost a quarter-century now. And our most recent research shows that the No. 1 thing on Christian teenagers' "church wish list" is to "learn more about Jesus." I love that. And this book is my way of throwing more wood on that fire. In these pages I hope your orbit comes so close to him that you can see him and taste him and smell him. When that happens, watch out....

COME TO JESUS

Practices, habits, and doables for changing the way you relate to Jesus

ASSUME WHAT YOU KNOW IS WRONG

We think we know Jesus, but we're wrong. Think of a person who seems to know Jesus really well—he (or she) is probably wrong about him. In our culture we're now at a place where we're so comfortable with Jesus, so confident of who he is and what he's like, that a lot of what we think we know is actually *wrong*. At a small conference I stood up and told a well-respected church consultant that her assertion that we all pretty much know all we need to know about Jesus was wrong. She disagreed with me, and I disagreed back. Our little interchange created a stir in the group—several people excitedly stopped me at the break. One of them said, "What all people—young and old—are *really* hungry for today is Jesus." I saw the same excited twinkle in his eye that I have when I talk about Jesus.

The first step in living a more Jesus-centered life is to assume that much of what you think you know about Jesus is wrong. It's time to wipe the whiteboard clean and start over, as if you've never heard of him. I've been assuming everything I know about Jesus is wrong for so many years now that I've slowly moved toward a life that orbits around a Jesus who is undeniably true. It has changed who I am, and it's revolutionized my impact on others. It will change you, too.

RELEASE YOUR INNER DEMOLITION EXPERT

Psychologists say that all of us hold on to "mental models" of the people we know. Because of the overwhelming amount of information our brains must organize, we tend to defend the established way we see something or someone. Even when we get new information that challenges our mental model, we hang on to what we've come to believe is the truth.[3] We do this same thing, obviously, with Jesus. But a great example of what this looks like is Richard Jewell, a central figure in the Centennial Olympic Park bombing at the 1996 Summer Olympics in Atlanta, Georgia.

Jewell was working as a private security guard when he discovered a pipe bomb, alerted the police, and helped to evacuate the area before it went off. In the media he was initially celebrated as a hero. But the FBI later grew suspicious of Jewell and leaked information that pointed to him as a suspect. Even though he was never charged with a crime, the "cloud of suspicion" around Jewell gave people a "mental model" of him as a terrorist bomber—most judged him as guilty, no matter what the truth was. That was true even after the real bomber—radical anti-abortion terrorist Eric Rudolph—actually *admitted* to the crime.[4]

This mental-model dynamic explains why so few of us have an accurate understanding of Jesus. Once our understanding of Jesus is established as a "mental model," we tend to ignore or tune out new information that doesn't fit the model. One way we can get rid of our mental models of Jesus is to blow them up, as if we were demolition experts. Ask these three questions whenever you read anything about Jesus in the Bible:

- What did Jesus *really* say? (What was the context of his remarks—who was he speaking to, where was he speaking, and why was he speaking?)

- What did Jesus *really* do? (In the context of "normal behavior" in his culture, what impact did his actions have on those who heard him—both positive and negative?)

- How did people *really* experience Jesus? (What is the array of emotional reactions people had to Jesus, and why did they react that way?)

ASK THE ONLY QUESTION THAT MATTERS

"Who do you say that I am?" Jesus asks his disciples this question after he's fed a huge crowd with only a few loaves and fishes. After this miraculous experience, Jesus wants to know what others, and his closest friends, really think of him. So he first asks a safer question: *"Who do the people say I am?"* And his friends answer that others are guessing that he is John the Baptist or Elijah or Jeremiah (come back from the

dead), or *"one of the prophets"* (Matthew 16:13-20). And then he looks them full-faced and asks a much riskier question: *"But who do you say that I am?"* And Peter answers by declaring that Jesus is *"the Christ, the son of the living God."* Today, and every day after today, make this the first question you ask in the morning: "Who do I say that Jesus is today?"

4

DID HE OR DIDN'T HE?

Another way to deconstruct your mental model of Jesus and rebuild something more true in its place is to practice this simple habit—whenever you read something about Jesus in the Bible, ask yourself these two little questions:

1.   What did Jesus do?
2.   What didn't Jesus do?

Look for things Jesus embraced, advised, or did. Then think about the things he *didn't* do. For example, if you see that he healed people of sicknesses, you'll also notice that he didn't charge anyone a fee for healing them. The key is to train yourself to mentally apply the brakes whenever you read or hear anything about Jesus—to push back against "self-evident truths." Get used to thinking about the true Jesus all the time, everywhere.

GET A LITTLE RUINED

Like a Lay's® potato chip, once you've tasted the real Jesus you won't
settle for just one taste of him. You know you're getting hooked on Jesus
when you do what Peter did in the aftermath of Jesus' least popular
sermon (in John 6). When Jesus told the crowds they'd have to "eat
his flesh and drink his blood" to be truly close to him, the adoring
"followers" suddenly thought better of following him. They thought he
was talking about cannibalism or something, and Jesus refused to clarify
himself after they repeatedly questioned him. So they took off faster
than the bulls running through the streets of Pamplona, Spain. But then
Jesus turned to his best friends and asked them the humblest question
in history: *"You do not want to go away also, do you?"* And Peter shoots
back with the best-ever answer to Jesus' best-ever question: *"Lord, to
whom shall we go? You have words of eternal life. We have believed and
have come to know that You are the Holy One of God"* (John 6:66-69).

I love this scene more than any other in the Bible. Peter is saying,
essentially: "I don't understand what you just said or most things you
do, and this whole thing is often confusing to me, but you've ruined
me for you...*forever.*" Can you imagine what it would be like to be so
ruined for Jesus that even if you wanted to reject him you couldn't?
One way to get there is to practice "the art of slowing down." It's

simple, really—read the Bible (or any book about Jesus) *slowly*. Make sure you *truly understand* what's happening, and what it would be like to *actually* be in the scene you're reading, before you move on. Make understanding Jesus your top goal when you read the Bible, not covering a lot of verses or chapters.

JESUS IS THE DEFINITION

Jesus rescued a tax collector named Matthew from a life of betrayal and cheating, and Matthew later writes about a man Jesus met who was even more lost than he was, but didn't know it. Here's the first part of the story of the Rich Young Ruler in Matthew 19: *And someone came to Him and said, "Teacher, what good thing shall I do that I may obtain eternal life?" And He said to him, "Why are you asking Me about what is good? There is only One who is good; but if you wish to enter into life, keep the commandments."*

Why would Jesus be so nitpicky about the man's use of the word *good*? I think it's because Jesus knows we use that word to describe so many things in our life that aren't actually *good* that he feels an intrinsic need to clarify what *good* actually is. And the definition of *good* is Jesus. His goodness—expressed in such divergent ways as his preoccupation with healing people and casting out their demons, to his tenderness for the broken and forgotten, to his ferocity directed toward the religious leaders of his day—is really the central aspect of his nature that we just don't "get."

Here's how to change the way you define *good* in your life. Whenever you think about Jesus or read about Jesus or talk about Jesus, remind yourself that whatever he's saying or doing is the deepest kind of good there is—no matter what it is.

WHEN YOU'RE BAKING A CAKE, DON'T FORGET THE FLOUR

Donald Miller, author of *Blue Like Jazz*, says he once conducted an experiment in a Bible college class he was teaching: He told his students he was going to explain the basics of the gospel message to them but would leave out one crucial truth. He challenged them to pick out the missing truth. He conducted his experiment by talking about humanity's sinfulness and examples of depravity in our culture, our need to repent because the wages of sin is death, the beauty of morality and the great hope of heaven, and all the great things we can experience once we're saved from the consequences of our sin.

But in Miller's class, not a single one of his students pointed out that "Jesus" was the missing "crucial truth." Miller writes: "I presented a gospel to Christian Bible college students and left out Jesus. Nobody noticed....⁵" It's hard to fathom, but it's possible to live out your "Christian" life and never really think about Jesus—and he's the main ingredient in the recipe! It seems funny, but when you've grown used to baking cakes without the flour, it takes a proactive act of remembering to make sure you put it in the mix. Otherwise, you'll have to settle for eating "flat-cake" the rest of your life. Here's something simple: Every time you eat or bake or see something made with flour, remind yourself of who is the "main ingredient" in your life.

COME AS YOU ARE, NOT AS YOU SHOULD BE

Most people are sheltering either a hidden past or a harrowing present—they have pain in their lives that even their best friends don't know about. And those hidden pains and struggles make many of us believe we're unacceptable to God. We feel like damaged goods. We've been told that our goal in life is to "accept" Jesus and convince others to "accept" Jesus (a term, incidentally, that's not even in the Bible) but it's ironic that we so often forget that God *accepts us already*, brokenness and all.

In John 4 we're told that Jesus broke the law, at least the law of social convention, when he sat alone with a "Samaritan-gone-wild" woman at a well. If anyone was ever "damaged goods," it was this woman. So Jesus sends his disciples into town ostensibly to buy food, but from the context it appears that he wanted to connect with this woman alone. The way that Jesus engaged this lonely, outcast woman is astounding. First, he initiates a relationship. Then he moves from connecting to honoring her by pursuing her and offering her hope. She wasn't a "ministry target"—his treatment of her demonstrated that he saw her as a precious daughter of his Father. As Jesus drew her into a real relationship, she sensed she could finally open up about her life. Real relationship with him starts when we come as we are, not as we should be. Have you admitted to Jesus who you really are? Or are you coming to him as the person you think you *should* be? Today is the day to change that game.

9

FIND A BIGGER "YES"

Most of us settle for what we can get in life, but Jesus is offering us the chance to say yes to something epic. My friend Greg Stier, founder of the Dare 2 Share ministry organization, once told me about the time he was standing in line at Starbucks® when he noticed a guy dressed like a goth staring at him with hate-filled eyes. Greg realized this guy had been reading the titles of the "Jesus books" he had under his arm. The guy asked, "Hey man, are you religious?" And Greg thought for a second, then responded, "I can't stand religious people—they make me want to puke." And the surprised goth-guy, now full of angry energy, said: "I can't stand them either! They think they're better than everybody else!" And then Greg shot back, "Do you know who else couldn't stand them?" And the guy asked, "Who?" And Greg delivered the coup de grace: "Jesus!"

The guy looked shocked by Greg's answer. So Greg explained: "I'm dead serious. As a matter of fact, Jesus, the Son of God, came down from heaven to hang out with sinners like you and me, but the religious people got mad so they crucified him. But Jesus had the last laugh. Three days later he rose again from the dead, proving that he was God. Now he offers sinners like you and me eternal life if we simply trust in him." By the time Greg had finished, this kid raised his fist into the air and shouted, "Jesus is awesome!"

After Greg told me this story, he followed it with this profound truth: "People need a much bigger 'Yes!' to overwhelm all the little 'No's' floating around in their brains." Jesus certainly offered his disciples a "bigger yes." Ever wonder why grown men in the middle of long-practiced careers would literally drop everything and risk their livelihood to start following an obscure "prophet"? The answer, I think, is in "I will make you fishers of men." He gave them a bigger "Yes!" Ask him for your bigger "Yes!" and he will give it to you.

10

OH COME LET ME ADORE HIM

The celebrated Christian writer Henri Nouwen served for years as pastor of Daybreak, a Christian community near Toronto for developmentally disabled people that was planted by the L'Arche movement. Nouwen had great respect for the co-founder of the L'Arche community in the United

States, Father George Strohmeyer. He tells this story about discovering the "secret ingredient" in Father Strohmeyer's life:

> George has always come to know Jesus with a depth, a richness that few priests have experienced. When he pronounces the name of Jesus you know that he speaks from a deep, intimate encounter.... I know for sure that there is a long and hard journey ahead of me. It is the journey of leaving everything behind for Jesus' sake. I now know that there is a way of living, praying, being with people, caring, eating, drinking, sleeping, reading, and writing in which Jesus is truly the center. I know this way exists and that I have not fully found it yet.
>
> How do I find it? George gave me the answer: "Be faithful in your adoration." He *did not* say "prayer," or "meditation," or "contemplation." He kept using the word "adoration," worship. This word makes it clear that all my attention must be on Jesus, not on myself. To adore is to be drawn away from my own preoccupations into the presence of Jesus. It means letting go of what I want, desire, or have planned, and fully trusting Jesus and his love.[6]

It's not possible to "adore" someone you know very little about. Adoration is the fruit of paying attention to something truly beautiful, and we don't pay very close attention to most of the truly beautiful things in our life. Learn something new about Jesus every day, no matter how small or insignificant the "new" seems to you, and you will find yourself adoring him very soon.

HIT EVERY POTHOLE

It seems strange, but if you want to get closer to Jesus and learn more about what makes him tick, look for the things he said and did that are hard to understand—I call them "Jesus potholes." For example, why did Jesus treat the Canaanite woman who was asking him for help in Matthew 15 so harshly? Or why, in John 7, did Jesus tell his brothers he wasn't going to attend a feast in Judea and then later go anyway? The key to "pothole-ing" is to ask yourself a simple question every time you come across something about Jesus that's hard to understand: "What's my best guess as to why Jesus said or did this?" Then don't give up until you answer your question. Think of yourself as a miner drilling deep into the earth because you're looking for gold. You really want that gold, so don't give up easily.

12

REMEMBERING TO REMEMBER

Throughout history the people of God, including you and me, have had a super-hard time remembering to remember God. I mean, we're following him, growing closer to him, and living our lives with him as our orbital center—and then we aren't. We forget all about who he really is and what he really does. Sure, I saw him come through for me yesterday, but I'm acting like he's my enemy today. You could say remembering to remember God is the primary spiritual discipline of our lives, because we're so typically bad at remembering to remember.

13

LEAVING KINDERGARTEN

There are two paths to growing in our relationship with Jesus—both are legitimate paths, but one of them goes "deeper into the woods," so to speak. The first path is to learn to trust in Jesus because of what he's done in the past—to remember the ways he's come through for you and others. On this path, our relationship with him is based on his track record and on our expectation that he'll continue to get a pretty good "grade." I think this is a kindergarten approach to a relationship— nothing wrong with it, but it's a little baby-ish. Going "deeper into the woods" means learning to trust Jesus not because of his track record, but because of what you've learned about who he is by "tasting and seeing" that he is good (Psalm 34:8). Many, many before us have walked this path, including Job and Abraham and David in the Old Testament, all the disciples in the New Testament, and billions more since then. Think of the person in your life who's impacted your life with Christ most profoundly. That person has likely gone "deep into the woods." Be that person for someone else.

BEELINING YOUR LIFE

As I mentioned in the introduction to this little book, a "beelined" life is a life that orbits around Jesus in every way possible. For example, who doesn't want to do well on a test at school or work toward a promotion at their job? But what would it look like to do these things because you're pursuing a closer relationship with Jesus? When we "give what we have to give" in every area of our life, we honor the way Jesus has wired us and the unique role he's created us to fill. The "because" of our life is, really, everything. Once you find out a person's because, you know most everything you need to know about him or her. So, do you know your because? Make it Jesus, and you'll be living a beelined life.

COME WITH A BLANK SLATE

Try this experiment on a day when you have a little more time than usual to read. Choose one of the four Gospels (Matthew, Mark, Luke, or John) and quickly read through it looking only for patterns in what Jesus said and did. You're not reading, necessarily, to understand everything he said and did—you're reading to experiment with a kind of hypothesis. You're testing something to see what you can learn from the test. As you quickly read, make a simple list of the things you observe as you're paying attention to what Jesus said and did. When you're finished, spend a little time answering this question: "If this is basically what Jesus said and did, how does my list challenge my previous perceptions of him?" Here's one from my list: "Jesus spent more time praying than speaking. Why?"

ACT LIKE JESUS MEANT WHAT HE SAID

In his excellent book *Jesus Mean and Wild*, Mark Galli describes a startling encounter with an unmasked Jesus. Galli was pastor of a California church when a group of Laotian refugees asked if they could become members. Galli offered to lead them through a study of the Gospel of Mark as a foundational exercise before they made their commitment. The Laotians had little knowledge of Scripture or of Jesus. When Galli got to the passage where Jesus calms the storm, he asked the refugees to talk about the "storms" in their lives—their problems, worries, and struggles. The people looked confused and puzzled. Galli filled the awkward silence by asking, "So what are your storms?" Finally, one of the Laotian men asked, "Do you mean that Jesus actually calmed the wind and sea in the middle of a storm?"

Galli thought the man was merely expressing his skepticism, and since he wasn't intending to spend the group's remaining time wrestling with the plausibility of Jesus' miracles, he said: "Yes, but we should not get hung up on the details of the miracle. We should remember that Jesus can calm the storms in our lives." After another uncomfortable stretch of silence, another man spoke up: "Well, if Jesus calmed the wind and the waves, he must be a very powerful man!" The Laotians buzzed with excitement about this while Galli looked on as a virtual outsider. While these newbie Christian refugees entered into something like worship, Galli realized he'd so taken Jesus for granted that he'd missed him altogether.[7]

Have you and I made the same mistake as Galli? Have we so taken Jesus for granted in our lives that we've essentially stopped relating with him as if he really did the things he did? Instead of making Jesus' words and actions into safer metaphors, how about we do something radical and simply accept what he said and did at face value, like we would do with any good friend?

17

STOP AT EVERY QUESTION

Jesus used great questions to teach his followers how to think critically and biblically. My friend Bob Krulish, the director of pastoral staff at my church in Denver, once scoured all four Gospels to extract every single question Jesus asked—and ended up with an astonishing 287 questions! And what explosive questions Jesus asked—so potent with little thought-bombs:

- *"If a man receives circumcision on the Sabbath that the Law of Moses may not be broken, are you angry with Me because I made an entire man well on the Sabbath?"* (John 7:23).

- *"Simon, son of John, do you truly love Me more than these?"* (John 21:15).

- *"Which is easier to say to the paralytic, 'Your sins are forgiven,' or to say, 'Get up, take your mat and walk?'"* (Mark 2:9).

When you read or hear about a question that Jesus asked, treat it like a stop sign. Stop, pay attention, look both ways, and decide how that question helps you understand Jesus better—what he likes and dislikes, promotes and discourages.

REMAIN IN JESUS

Experiences and habits that gently lure you into a dependent relationship with Jesus

PAY ATTENTION TO THE PARABLES IN YOUR LIFE

In a portion of Romans 1:19-20, Paul says this startling truth: *That which is known about God is evident within them; for God made it evident to them. For since the creation of the world His invisible attributes, His eternal power and divine nature, have been clearly seen, being understood through what has been made.* Paul is saying that all we need to know about God is already evident, if we'll just pay attention. That means God has embedded parables and metaphors—stories or symbols that teach a truth about him—all around us, to help us get to know him as he is. So, if we pay better attention to those parables and symbols, recognizing them for what they are, we'll come to know Jesus more intimately.

It's a simple practice, once you decide to pay attention. You simply notice what you notice in your everyday life and then ask God if it's a parable or a metaphor for something true about him or his kingdom. For example, one day I was driving down the highway during rush hour and saw a bunch of papers swirling around—getting chewed up in the traffic. I passed an off-ramp, where I saw a guy getting out of his car to grab the last few sheets of paper stuck on the back of his car—he'd obviously stacked his important papers on his car when he left home, then forgot they were there. I asked God if this scene was a parable or symbol for something true about him or his kingdom. What surfaced in my head was that this was a picture of the consequences of my sin: I can be forgiven, but like that paper scattered all over the highway, I can't keep the effects of my sin from spreading—I can't get that consequence back. This is everyday parable-mining.

DETERMINE TO KNOW NOTHING

Dr. David Walsh, founder and president of the National Institute on Media and Family, has a motto: "Whoever tells the stories defines the culture." And right now, says Walsh, the storytellers are defining our culture by teaching us that these should be our primary values:

- More

- Fast

- Easy

- Fun[8]

It's no wonder that so many of us see Jesus through these filters. We want him to give us more of what we want, to make things fast and easy for us, and we want guarantees that our fun won't be compromised if we follow him. This is why Spurgeon's beeline is such a crucial guide and metaphor—if we "beeline" everything we do back to Jesus, we might have a shot at remembering him for who he is. Put another way, if our primary pursuit, like the Apostle Paul's, is to "determine to know nothing but Christ, and him crucified," we'll naturally develop a countercultural mindset about our life. How can we believe (for too long) that life is about "more, fast, easy, and fun" when we're determined to pursue our deepening relationship with Jesus above all else?

20

PRACTICE CONGRUENCE

At the heart of a life that orbits around Jesus is something called "practicing congruence." I first heard "congruence" described as a crucial life practice over breakfast one morning with my pastor, Tom Melton. "Congruence," he said, "is when you're the same person—with the same priorities, passions, and personality—in every arena in your life. When you're not spending energy adapting yourself to every competing arena, you have a lot more energy to make an impact in those arenas. It means living on the outside what is true on the inside."

Essentially, a congruent life means *what you say is who you are, in every environment*, and it's evident from your choices and priorities. You make a conscious decision to maintain who you are in all the settings of your life. It's not easy at first, but pretty soon you'll get the hang of it and it'll be hard to go back to living in incongruence. When you're congruent, you create something like a gravitational center that exerts unseen "pull" on the people within that gravitational field. And when your life is congruent around a passion for Christ, you tend to draw others into that orbit.

TAKE NOTHING

When Jesus decided to send out his disciples two-by-two, for the first time preaching and healing and casting out demons without him by their side, he made a daunting task even more challenging. He told them that they were not allowed to bring extra money or a change of clothes, or arrange where they would stay at night ahead of time. They could take nothing with them but the clothes on their back—forcing them to depend upon God for everything. And that's just the way Jesus wanted it—radical dependence. Today, what are you depending on for your life? Pause and answer that question for yourself. Then, just for today, decide to depend upon God for what you need instead of your normal "go-to" resources, whatever they are. When you live more consciously dependent upon God, big stuff happens, and your dependence helps you to draw closer to Jesus.

22

MAKE PRAYER LIKE PLAY

In his book *Prayer*, Philip Yancey describes prayer as an adventurous partnership with God—in prayer we saddle up and ride with him on his great mission to rescue those he loves.[9] But prayer, for most of us, is more like an arduous discipline. We work at it—see, even the language we use to describe prayer betrays our true feelings about it. It's a discipline we must muster and master to get God to do what we want him to do. But when prayer is more like play we don't pray only at certain times, with certain words, in certain places, and in a certain tone of voice. Instead, we *converse* with God about the people and concerns that are most important to us. Here's my favorite way to turn prayer into play. Before I pray for myself, or for someone else, I always pause (even if just for 10 seconds) to ask God first: "How would you like me to pray for the person or thing I'm praying about?" Then I wait until it feels like I have some kind of direction from God—it could be a word or a picture or a Bible story or passage or really anything—and then I pray based upon what I've sensed. This has radically changed the way I pray, and it's made prayer a fun adventure instead of an arduous task. I know it will change your whole approach to prayer as well and make your conversations with God much more electric.

ASK JESUS TO GROW WHEAT, NOT PULL WEEDS

Marcus Buckingham and Donald Clifton, authors of the bestselling business book *Now Discover Your Strengths*, popularized a profound truth that can have a far-reaching impact on our lives. It's a truth that's locked up in a strange little story Jesus told—the parable of the wheat and weeds in Matthew 13. In it, Jesus tells about a man who sowed good wheat in his field, but an enemy came at night and also sowed weeds in the field. The servants want to pull up the weeds, but the farmer says no, because they'll also pull up good wheat.

Jesus is essentially saying, "Don't pay attention to the bad stuff—the weeds; instead, concentrate on nurturing the good stuff. I'll take care of the bad stuff later on." Buckingham and Clifton make the case that the best way to manage people in a business setting is to discover their strengths and fuel them, not look for their weaknesses and try to remove or improve them. Organizations that shift their attention from trying to attack their workers' weaknesses and instead concentrate on fueling their strengths, experience remarkable success.[10] In your life and in your prayers, spend more time asking God to fuel the wheat in your life, and trust him to take care of the weeds.

24

THE NAME YOU EMBRACE IS THE NAME YOU BECOME

In Matthew 16:18, Jesus tells Peter, after his closest friend has declared that he is *"the Christ, the son of the living God,"* this remarkable secret: *"I also say to you that you are Peter, and upon this rock I will build My church; and the gates of Hades will not overpower it."* Jesus is revealing to Peter that he and his Father and the Holy Spirit have their own name for him—and it's not the one Peter's parents gave him. It's the name "Rock" ("Petros," or Peter), and it had never before been used as a name for someone. What this tells us is that it's more than likely that all of us have a name given to us by God that is not the name our parents gave us. It's a name that has our purpose and true identity embedded in it. And so, it's natural for us to ask God to reveal to us the name he calls us by. I do this almost every day: "Jesus, who do you say that I am?" There is no more important question in my life, or in yours.

25

DO, OR DO NOT—THERE IS NO TRY

In *The Empire Strikes Back*, when Luke Skywalker is trying his best to master that mysterious Jedi ability called The Force, he tells his mentor

Yoda that he's trying as hard as he can. And Yoda replies: "Do, or do not—there is no try." It's a goofy example, but there is truth in it for our life with Jesus. We reflect the spirit of Jesus when we substitute "I'm doing" for "I'm trying" in our lives, and we more truly live on the razor's edge of faith when we *believe and do* than when we calculate our odds and merely try hard.

NOTHING IS BENEATH PRAYER

Talk with God about everything, not just some things. I call this the "parking space prayer imperative." You know how we look down on praying for insignificant things like a good parking space or a short line at the movie theater? These things, we say, are too trivial to bother God with—we're too self-centered anyway. But I think the truth is just the opposite—God is at least as passionately interested in the details of my life as my family is, so if my focus is riveted on getting a good parking space for some reason, why wouldn't I talk to God about that? God wants to be involved in every aspect of my life—nothing is too small for his concern and consultation.

KICK AT THE DARKNESS 'TIL IT BLEEDS DAYLIGHT

I find it magnetic, humbling, and profound that Jesus spent so much time retreating from the crowds, his friends, his family—everyone—to spend intimate time with his Father. *But Jesus often withdrew to lonely places and prayed (Luke 5:16 NIV).* Jesus often proclaimed that he was "one" with his Father—how did he know? Well, because he'd spent an eternity talking with and laughing with and strategizing with and enjoying his Father—alone.

I love this Bruce Cockburn lyric from his song "Lovers in a Dangerous Time":

> When you're lovers in a dangerous time
>
> Sometimes you're made to feel as if your love's a crime
>
> But nothing worth having comes without some kind of fight
>
> Got to kick at the darkness 'til it bleeds daylight[11]

Intimacy with God is a prize that will cost you everything to claim. The currents are propelling us toward a shallow life of meaning and relationships. Time alone with God is like a paddle in your hand—giving you the ability to move against the current.

A friend of mine once told me: "The biggest challenge is knowing Jesus intimately enough to describe him to others—and we've got a lot going on that's keeping us from knowing him intimately." Amen.

LIVE "THE PROGRESSION"

My friend Ned Erickson once shared with me something he calls "The Progression." Following it has changed my life. If you follow it you will see your life change as well. It goes like this: "Get to know Jesus well, because the more you know him, the more you'll love him, and the more you love him, the more you'll want to follow him, and the more you follow him, the more you'll become like him, and the more you become like him, the more you become yourself."[12]

PRACTICE YOUR DESPERATION

There's a lot we can learn from the ragged, fringe-y people who were drawn to Jesus, and vice versa. They were desperate for rescue in their lives, and therefore they saw Jesus for who he really is: a rescuer. The funny thing is, the closer you get to Jesus the more he will put you in situations that make you even more desperate for him. Sounds a little scary, but it's actually the most fulfilling way to live your life. When Jesus was sending his disciples out on a challenging and demanding ministry journey, he gave them these parting words: *"Freely you have received, freely give. Do not take along any gold or silver or copper in your belts; take no bag for the journey, or extra tunic, or sandals or a staff; for the worker is worth his keep" (Matthew 10:8b-10).* Rather than depend on your own strength and resources, Jesus is inviting you to depend on him. That's what's called "an abundant life."

30

ATTACH INSTEAD OF APPLY

When you closely examine what Jesus really has to say about family relationships, you discover he's not as "family-friendly" as we've all been led to believe. Here's a passage to chew on, in Matthew 10:34-39 (NIV): *"Do not suppose that I have come to bring peace to the earth. I did not come to bring peace, but a sword. For I have come to turn 'a man against his father, a daughter against her mother, a daughter-in-law against her mother-in-law—a man's enemies will be the members of his own household.'"* Jesus respects our DNA family, but he also expands it to include all who commit their lives to him. Jesus compares the people who've given their lives to him to a branches grafted into a Vine—he's made it possible for us to "receive adoption" into his family. But this is no normal adoption—we're not only invited into the Family (the Father, Son, and Holy Spirit), he also makes it possible for us be "blood brothers and sisters." Our life is, therefore, not about trying harder and harder to deserve our status as family members, but simply doing all we can to stay attached to Jesus—the branch "abiding" in the Vine.

31

JESUS IS THE HEADWATERS

Luke records Jesus sending out 72 of his followers to heal people and cast out demons. When they return they say, *"Lord, even the demons submit to us in your name."* And Jesus jumps in to make sure they remember where that authority really comes from: *"I saw Satan fall like lightning from heaven. I have given you authority to trample on snakes and scorpions and to overcome all the power of the enemy; nothing will harm you. However, do not rejoice that the spirits submit to you, but rejoice that your names are written in heaven"* (Luke 10:17-20 NIV). Jesus is basically reminding them that the power they experienced on their adventure came directly from him (so they shouldn't get too impressed with themselves) and the power to cast out demons is nothing compared to the reality that God had adopted them into his family. Jesus is simply using a powerful experience as the context to teach and frame the truth: If we have good things flowing through our lives, we can trace that stream back to its headwaters, which is Jesus himself.

32

PRACTICE AMOS 5:4

I often wonder about the balance between trusting Jesus for something in my life and the responsibility I have to "make it happen." Once, I asked my friend Bob Krulish about this, because he's an older and wiser follower of Christ. And he laughed at my question, his eyes sparkling. And then he said, simply: "Rick, it's all about Amos 5:4." And I knew immediately what he was trying to say to me, because Bob often reminds me of Amos 5:4. It reads: "Seek God and live." Bob was trying to remind me that a life with God isn't about following formulas and principles—it's about following Jesus. When we're challenged by something in life, we seek God about it, and then do what we sense he's asking us to do. That's a relationship. And that's what he's always wanted with us.

33

INVITE THE IRON

In Proverbs 27:17 the wise King Solomon writes: *Iron sharpens iron, so one man sharpens another."* If you think about it, getting "sharpened" by others in your life probably doesn't feel so great. It hurts to have someone cut into you for the purpose of sharpening your "blade." I create ministry workshops for youth pastors, and our creative process from start to finish is characterized by what I call "wood-chipper" moments. In other words, after I've planned a workshop, our creative team gets together to chop it up for a couple of hours. It's brutal—"brutal for good." We chip away at it, again and again, until it's what we all want. I often create 10 versions of the workshop before it's all over. We'd never get to this point if I were a pansy about "iron sharpening iron." Well, I *have* been a pansy about it sometimes. But now I've developed a strange aversion to wimpy criticism: "Come on, give me your best shot." The more you are open to the "iron" in your life, the more likely you are to move your life from good to great.

THERE IS NO "USE;" THERE IS ONLY "WITH"

Christians often say or pray something like this: "I just want God to use me." But the truth is, no loving father would ever say, "My mission is to *use* my kids as much as I can." Instead, our Good Father longs for us to be companions on his great adventure—the adventure of the redemption of the world. We're not merely useful to him. God loves us and wants us to grow into who we really are. John Wooden, hall-of-fame coach of the great UCLA basketball teams in the 1960s, made his players *both* better people and better basketball players. That word got out to every basketball player in America. Because he "took care of his players," he didn't even have to recruit. Everyone wanted to come and be with him. You'll never find God "using" people in Scripture, but you will find God partnering with them, moving through them, fighting alongside them, and commissioning them. Those are great (and true) words to express our Jesus-centered hopes.

REFLECT JESUS

Activities, projects, and surprising ways to deconstruct the false Jesus embraced in our culture and replace that façade with the real Jesus

GIVE WHAT YOU HAVE TO GIVE

Not long ago I was talking with Ron Belsterling, a professor at Nyack College in New York, about an experience he had when he was pursuing his doctoral degree. Ron convinced a church to experiment with an outreach trip that targeted a nearby inner-city neighborhood instead of the youth group's traditional overseas trip that included four days of "ministry" and six days of fun on the beach. Parents who were fine about their kids going on a cross-cultural mission/fun trip were very worried about them walking the streets of an urban neighborhood that was just 20 minutes away.

One night Ron and the kids on his inner-city outreach looked out the window of their hotel and saw two men viciously kicking a woman who was high on drugs, and therefore unable to defend herself or run away. Ron turned to these protected, wide-eyed, middle-class kids and asked, "What are we going to do about this?"

The kids said, "Well, we can't go down there!"

Ron answered, "Why not? *Down there* is where Jesus would be."

The kids responded: "What can we do? The only thing we know how to do is sing!" (Most of the kids on the outreach were part of the church's respected youth choir.)

Ron fired back, "Well, let's go down there and sing, then. We'll give what Jesus has given us to give."

So the whole group trooped down to the street, stood on the opposite sidewalk, and started singing. The two guys kicking the woman looked up, startled, and then immediately ran away in fear. The woman then crawled across the street and lay down in the middle of the kids as they continued singing. That night, those kids followed the beeline that Ron found for them—they learned what it's like to be rescuers, just like Jesus. And the wall separating their faith from their real life crumbled a little more.

36

OFFER RIDICULOUS LOVE FOR YOUR ENEMIES

When parents and friends and siblings are acting less like our neighbors and more like our enemies, that's a glorious opportunity to behave like Jesus and give evidence that we're sons and daughters of a God who "causes the rain to fall on the just and the unjust." Jesus said it's basically a no-brainer to love the people who love you—the real evidence that you're one of his brothers or sisters is that you love the people who don't particularly love you.

37

SCARE YOURSELF

Jesus-centered living is all about doing the sometimes-scary things God asks us to do because we're never more alive than when we're following him on a new adventure. It might mean we serve in a leadership role for a ministry event, or it might mean serving others in a setting that's far outside our comfort zone, or it might mean reaching out to people whose problems are beyond our ability to solve. Our life, simply, is about getting out of our "boat" (the expected life) and walking on water (the unexpected life). We don't do this because we can walk on water; we do it because God has asked us to walk on water. It's his responsibility to keep us afloat.

38

ARE YOU TASK-FOCUSED OR PEOPLE-FOCUSED?

Are you a "people over task" person or a "task over people" person? No matter what tasks or responsibilities or activities you're involved in, do the people you're with experience more of Christ because of their involvement with you? Or do they feel pressured, frenetic, stressed, chaotic, and tense because of their involvement with you? When Jesus is on his way to heal the gravely ill daughter of a synagogue official named Jairus, when every second counts, Jesus stops to engage a woman who'd found healing from a terrible illness when she touched his garment. He pays attention to her story, even though a sick girl is going to die because of his delay. He later raises that girl from the dead, but the message here is that always, every person's story matters. Today, will the people in your life sense their stories matter to you?

39

PRACTICE NOT-SO-CRAZY TALK

The best guitar players started by learning chords—the basic building blocks of music. Some guitar-playing websites promise to teach willing students to "play like Clapton" in 30 days. But online guitar teacher Danny Poole scoffs at those claims: "Eric Clapton didn't learn how to play like Eric Clapton in 30 days….What most people don't realize is that there are no quick fixes when it comes to playing the guitar, or any instrument." The more Clapton practiced, the better he sounded. And the more you talk about Jesus with friends and family—in natural, conversational ways—the more you'll feel relaxed doing it.

40

PRACTICE EXTREME GENEROSITY

Do we serve and give to people because we're hoping they will, in turn, follow Christ or (more fundamentally) give us something we want in return? If so, we're merely practicing "transactional" giving: I give because I get. But Jesus was never a transactional giver. Think of the number of times he healed people or cast out demons from them without saying a word about committing their lives to him. Often, the most he got was a "thank you" for what he'd given them, and sometimes not even that. *The man who was healed had no idea who it was, for Jesus had slipped away into the crowd that was there (John 5:13 NIV).* Extreme generosity is giving the way Jesus gave—with no requirement that you receive anything in return.

41

DON'T TALK BEFORE YOU'VE LISTENED

Before you offer advice to someone, make sure you've listened well first. Jesus studied people the same way Sherlock Holmes studied clues. If we're channeling Jesus or Sherlock, we'll always be trying to unlock a person's reality by listening with unusual attention. Think of the people around you as mysteries you're trying to solve. Challenge yourself to enter into every conversation with a mission to pay attention to people more closely than the rest of humanity does. It's as simple as noticing when one of your outgoing friends is uncharacteristically quiet, then asking if that friend is struggling with something. Pay way more attention to details than you have before, then follow your gut and ask questions based on what you observe or sense. It's arrogant—and un-Jesus-like—to assume we know best how to advise someone when we haven't listened well first.

GO INTO THE CAVE

How did Jesus enter into the stories of others? When he was told that his good friend Lazarus had died while he was on the way to heal him, the Bible says Jesus was "deeply moved, troubled, and weeping." Our mission in entering into another's difficult story is to prove that we are with them, to remind them of who God is, and to remind them of who they really are. I call this "going into the cave" on behalf of others. It comes from a scene in the film *The Return of the King*—the hero Aragorn saddles his horse for a trip down the Dimholt Road to visit an army of dead people who "live" under a mountain. His mission is to give them a chance to repent for a long-ago betrayal by joining his army in the war against the evil enemy Sauron. The elf Legolas and the dwarf Gimli insist on going with Aragorn. They arrive at the dark entrance to the mountain, where a sign warns them that no one escapes the mountain alive. Aragorn plunges in anyway, saying, "I do not fear death." His commitment to his friends requires him to risk death on their behalf—to go into the cave on their behalf.

One way to go into the cave on behalf of others is to do what I call "asking the next question." It simply means training yourself to keep asking questions of your friends until you get a "real" answer. Most people give up on a line of questioning before they get to breakthrough. Relax about awkward silence, wait, or ask the question in another way. Keep asking follow-up questions until you get close to what's really going on in your friend's life.

43

ANSWER THE ONLY THREE QUESTIONS THAT MATTER

I love what Steve Merritt, a longtime columnist for Group Magazine, says about "going into the cave" after others. Merritt is a counselor, and he says: "As a counselor I meet with cynical, skeptical, scared, and hurt teenagers every day, and each one asks the same three questions: 1. Do you understand me? 2. Are you going to be real, or are you like the rest of the imposters in the world? 3. Do you care?"[13] If you can answer these three questions with "yes," your friends will most likely open up their real life to you.

TREAT EVERY STORY LIKE IT'S THE GREATEST STORY

Here's an irony: At a time when more and more people are disconnected from each other, the number of celebrity magazines is climbing. Our curiosity is misplaced—we feed our fascination for almost-silly celebrity details but we largely ignore the riveting stories of "average" people. Of course, we're drawn to powerful stories, but we don't always recognize them in the people who surround us in everyday life. God is writing *every* person's story—creating beauty out of ugliness whenever it's offered to him. In a Jesus-centered friendship, both people move toward each other with unrelenting curiosity because, like Jesus, their primary purpose is to bring more glory to God by helping others become freer than they are now.

SET YOUR ALARM

Early in the 19th century, a Hungarian doctor named Ignaz Philipp Semmelweis discovered, almost by accident, that if he washed his hands between procedures, the percentage of patients who died after surgery dropped from 25 percent to almost nothing. But his hand-washing strategy was considered so ludicrous by the medical establishment that Semmelweis was fired from the hospital and later died at a young age, crazed with despair over the wholesale dismissal of his discovery. In his profile of Semmelweis, Dr. William C. Wood says, "I think there are… lessons to be learned from [his] life. The first is why there was such resistance to truth. People were too busy to investigate personally what he presented…The physicians of Semmelweis' day, with few exceptions, did not examine the facts firsthand."[14]

Our *first* responsibility as followers of Christ is to develop a firsthand critique about the common assumptions, beliefs, and practices of the culture we live in. For example, Jesus prodded his disciples to consider who was making the bigger sacrifice: the rich religious leaders who made a lot of noise when they gave out of their excess income, or the widow who put a penny into the temple offering even though it was all she had (Mark 12:41-44). Jesus was always questioning the conventional wisdom and common practices of his culture. And we're living close to him when we "push back" against the "givens" of our culture, comparing everything to the truths Jesus revealed about his kingdom. We ask these simple questions:

1. What's the overall message of this cultural influence, in one sentence?

2. What "truths" is it teaching?

3. What promises is it making?

4. Who's sending the message, and why?

5. Are these messages, truths, or promises that Jesus honors?

DESTROY THE PLANS OF THE DESTROYER

The Bible says Jesus came "to destroy the works of the devil." So, how are we supposed to do the same in our everyday lives? When was the last time you saw the work of a demon? Well, anytime you see a person's life threatened with destruction, or a lie that's treated like the truth, or an idol that's treated like God, or an addiction to a source of life that isn't God himself—you're seeing "the works of the devil." But what does it mean to "destroy" those things? The simplest expression is to bring light and truth into every situation—when Satan and his works are contended with, he flees. It happens over and over in the New Testament. Demonic influence is like the tape that blocks the finish line in a race—a runner can smash right through it if he'll simply keep running. So bring truth where there is a lie, and *resist the devil and he will flee from you (James 4:7).*

LIVE YOUR OWN MISSION IMPOSSIBLE

If ever there was an impossible dream, it was the redemption of sinful human beings. Our betrayal, through Adam and Eve, was a sure and permanent way to separate us from the love of God. So, was Jesus focused on us or on his Father when he agreed to leave heaven and enter into our world as a baby? If he were focused on us, the task ahead would've seemed overwhelming. I mean, just look at us. We're a mess, and there are a lot of us. But Jesus wasn't looking at us; he was staring at his Father the whole time: *Therefore Jesus answered and was saying to them, "Truly, truly, I say to you, the Son can do nothing of Himself, unless it is something He sees the Father doing; for whatever the Father does, these things the Son also does in like manner" (John 5:19).* The key to living your own mission impossible is to watch what the Father does, then do these things "in like manner."

PLAY ON JESUS' PLAYGROUND

What's the point of Jesus walking on water or feeding thousands of people with a few loaves and fishes or raising people from the dead or turning water into wine? And what does Jesus want us to know about him—and about his Father—through the supernatural things he does? Jesus is always and everywhere playfully reminding his close friends that, like Superman, he hails from another place. "This is how we do it on Krypton (also known as the kingdom of God)." Jesus is ultimately relaxed about "commanding mountains to move," because he sees the "natural" and the "supernatural" as different points on a continuum of everyday living. "The road less traveled" for Jesus is always the road to the swing set: He chooses a playful approach to problems, and that often translates to a supernatural approach. We "play" in his "playground" when we ask for his supernatural intervention and expect it to happen.

GIVE HOPE, KEEP NONE

One of the defining quotes in the last *Lord of the Rings* film, *The Return of the King*, comes in a powerful interchange between the elf king Elrond and the heroic king-to-be Aragorn. At a crucial tipping point in the story, when the odds are stacked against them and defeat seems sure, the two repeat an ancient creed of kings to each other: "I give hope to men; I keep none for myself." This is our rallying cry, the words that free us to move with courage in our lives.

50

FEED HIS SHEEP

After Jesus conquers death and returns to launch the disciples on their mission to advance the gospel, he asks Peter three times if he loves him, and after each "Yes, Lord," Jesus tells Peter how to live out his "yes"— "Feed my sheep." What does "feed my sheep" mean for you? Well, this is the way we *work out [our] salvation (Philippians 2:12)*. Each of us has something unique and beautiful to offer to the world. The real question is not, "Do you have food for my sheep?"—it's whether we'll offer the food he's given us to give.

51

FIND A DOABLE CHALLENGE

These twelve Jesus sent out with the following instructions: "Do not go among the Gentiles or enter any town of the Samaritans. Go rather to the lost sheep of Israel" (Matthew 10:5-6 NIV). Rather than forcing his disciples into a cross-cultural challenge or an environment that promised stiff resistance, Jesus starts them off in familiar surroundings with familiar people. Later on they'll go "to the ends of the earth," but for now the challenge needs to be small enough to ensure some level of success.

When I was learning how to be a street evangelist in Europe (even now I'm amazed I really did that when I was young), our trainers started us off by teaching us a discussion-starting drama we could perform to attract a crowd. The first place we did it was a public piazza in Rome that was well known as a gathering place for young people interested in conversation with Americans. We did the drama, and it provided an easy way to strike up a conversation with strangers. The bridge from shy, scared, awkward guy to international missionary was relatively easy because my leaders understood how to give us doable challenges. Find your doable challenge.

MATCH YOUR "HAVE" WITH THEIR "NEED"

"Whatever town or village you enter, search there for some worthy person and stay at their house until you leave. As you enter the home, give it your greeting. If the home is deserving, let your peace rest on it; if it is not, let your peace return to you. If anyone will not welcome you or listen to your words, leave that home or town and shake the dust off your feet" (Matthew 10:11-14 NIV). Not every person or place will welcome what you have to give. No problem. Keep giving what you have, expecting that some will like it and some won't. We're not called to only those who will respond well to what we have to give—we're called to give, and leave the rest to Jesus.

53

MAKE TROUBLE YOUR BADGE OF HONOR

Jesus warned his disciples: *"Be on your guard; you will be handed over to the local councils and be flogged in the synagogues" (Matthew 10:17 NIV).* When Capt. Chesley "Sully" Sullenberger realized he'd have to land his Airbus A320 on the Hudson River after a flock of geese destroyed both engines, the only thing he said to the passengers was "Brace for impact." He did not say, "No worries, I've got it all under control." Instead, he told them the plane was about to plunge onto the surface of an urban river, and they should ready themselves for a crash landing. Jesus does the very same thing with us, because he never candy-coats our reality. That's not ultimately comforting. He believes we can handle the truth, and the truth is that we will face trouble when we follow him.

54

JESUS ISN'T WORRIED ABOUT YOU

Jesus trusted his followers with huge responsibilities and refused to micromanage them because he wasn't scared by their potential failure. *After Jesus had finished instructing his twelve disciples, he went on from there to teach and preach in the towns of Galilee (Matthew 11:1 NIV).* Jesus delivers his marching orders to the disciples, then he takes off on his own ministry trip. Talk about communicating trust! Effectively, he's telling them he's not at all worried or anxious about how they would fare on their adventure. You can do great things in your life because Jesus isn't worried about you.

55

HIGHJACKING GRACE

Do you offer grace before your meals? How about surprising everyone, including yourself, with an alternative to the expected? What if you, instead, asked everyone to raise a glass to Jesus and then toasted him? Or what if you asked everyone to loudly whisper a cheer—"Jesus!"—all at the same time? Or what if you quoted a Jesus-centered Scripture passage such as Ephesians 3:20-21? *Now to Him who is able to do far more abundantly beyond all that we ask or think, according to the power that works within us, to Him be the glory in the church and in Christ Jesus to all generations forever and ever. Amen.* The point is to follow the beeline in everything we do.

56

YOUR JESUS SIGNATURE

When I return emails, I have a "signature" function that automatically gets added to the end of my messages. Every email I send includes this: "Be Christ's!" If you have the same feature, consider including a Jesus-centered message with your signature. For example: *"I have determined to know nothing but Jesus Christ, and him crucified."* Or if you're text messaging, consider signing each message with a Jesus-centered "icon" such as "4JC." Or come up with your own creative way to leave your "mark."

57

VOICE-MAILING IT IN

Consider changing your voice-mail message on your phone every week to include a very short statement in your message that replicates one of the "Beautiful Declarations" starting on page 65. For example, after your standard "I'm not here" message, simply close by saying "Courage rules the other virtues."

THE HOLY REJECTIONS

A series of ridiculously glorious everyday refusals

58

REJECT A REDUCED JESUS

In the foreword to Mark Galli's book *Jesus Mean and Wild*, author Eugene Peterson (paraphraser of *The Message* version of the Bible) writes: "Every omitted detail of Jesus, so carefully conveyed to us by the Gospel writers, reduces Jesus. We need the whole Jesus. The complete Jesus. Everything he said. Every detail of what he did."[15] A great life is always about a determination to not settle—and not settling for a partial or palatable or prissy Jesus will help unlock the door to the surprising, magnetic, and untamed Jesus. So, never skip over something he said or did. Instead, linger over his words and his stories until the fog of the false Jesus begins to clear.

59

REJECT WWJD

I have a personal skepticism about the "What Would Jesus Do?" movement—it's pretty much lost its steam now, and I'm not in mourning. I think there's a much worse acronym that is much more valuable for us to ask ourselves than WWJD, every day—it's DWKJWETKWHD. The letters stand for: *Do we know Jesus well enough to know what he'd do?* The evidence—in others and in us—says the answer is, clearly, "no." But there's great hope in embracing this "no" because when we do, we can pursue a deeper intimacy with Jesus before we assume we can guess what he'd do in any situation. And if we're asking ourselves DWKJWETKWHD all the time, then the natural progression is to make WDJD our primary focus—it stands for "What *Did* Jesus Do?" It's far more important to understand what Jesus *actually did* than ponder what he *might do* if he were in our shoes. WWJD can force us into a mental exercise that makes us distant observers of him, not relaters to him. But WDJD can draw us into a charged intimacy with Jesus. Have you had your WDJD moment today?

60

REJECT THE NICE JESUS

A church in North Carolina decided to satirize the "fake Jesus" most of us have come to know—to poke fun at our wrong notions of Jesus so we can see him with fresh eyes. They took an ancient and campy film about Jesus, extracted four scenes from it, and then recorded their own dialogue to replace the original audio. The result is hilarious—they gave Jesus a falsetto voice that sounds like the children's TV show host Mister Rogers, portraying him as the super-nice-guy Jesus so many of us imagine him as anyway. The false Jesus in these videos is painfully funny—it's a brilliant stroke of deconstruction to actually show the Jesus we have unwittingly believed in. And when that false Jesus is exposed, we're left hungering for a taste of the real thing.

REJECT A "SPOKE" RELATIONSHIP

According to a massive sociological study called the National Study of Youth and Religion, just 1 out of 10 Americans have what researchers call a "devoted" faith—that means:

- Their faith in Christ is central to their life.

- They know the basics of their faith.

- Their relationship with Jesus makes an impact in their everyday life.[16]

So, for almost everyone, Jesus is not at the hub of their life—he's either a "spoke" on their life's wheel (just a church thing) or not even that. They have no firm idea of who Jesus really is, why he came, what he actually said, what he actually did, or what he's doing now. And when something happens in their "real" world, they struggle to understand Jesus' connection to it. If this news is sobering, that's a good sign. Be different. If Jesus isn't even a spoke on your life's wheel, add a spoke. If he's already a spoke, treat him like he's the hub and see what happens. If he's already the hub of your life, remember to remember him.

REJECT LIP SERVICE

Sarcasm can be really funny—I'm pretty sarcastic myself, so I appreciate the "art form." But sarcasm has a dark side, too. I've noticed that a lot of Christ-followers use sarcasm to keep a safe distance between them and others, including Jesus. We'd rather reel off a witty joke about Jesus and the Christian life than live it with him. One way to draw nearer to Jesus, and to others, is to reject sarcasm and replace it with words that truly encourage or are funny without the cutting edge that characterizes sarcastic humor. That edge is designed to make it OK to keep Jesus waiting on the doorstep but never really invite him in to sleep on the couch in our living room. In Revelation 3:20 Jesus says this: *"Behold, I stand at the door and knock; if anyone hears My voice and opens the door, I will come in to him and will dine with him, and he with Me."* How long will we listen to the knock on the door before we lay down our sarcasm and invite him in?

REJECT YOUR COMFORTABLE LIFE

Guitarist Tim McTague of the band Underoath wrote this little manifesto for Jesus-centered living in CCM Magazine awhile back:

I believe that we, as Christians, have lost sight of what Christ intended our lives to be and the purpose and faith He gave His life to teach us. As long as we give our 39 cents a day and make it to church on Wednesday and Sunday, we're all good...the American way...the new "Christianity." Whatever happened to the church of Acts where people would sell all they had and give to the poor and join a body of thousands of people, living a life of prayer, community and servanthood?

We now sit, 2,000 years later, in our comfortable homes and Lexuses and mega-church youth groups watching the rest of the world rot away and starve to death. Where is Christ in our watered-down, self-serving hybrid of faith and hypocrisy...the new "Christianity"? God exists to pay our mortgages and heal our families, but, when it comes time to sacrifice something of our own, we look away.

Somewhere along the way, we decided that being a Christian wasn't a life of serving but a life of being served. You can change the world. God is real and is waiting for a few real Christians to step up and let Him work through them the way He worked through the disciples. But it will cost everything... This is no longer YOUR life...so stop living like it is.[17]

REJECT THE "GOOD PERSON" SYNDROME

Can good people earn eternal salvation through their good deeds? About 4 out of 10 teenagers say this is true. This single belief—that life is about becoming a better and better person so that we deserve heaven at the end of it all—is the most damaging false belief we have. Remember the lesson of the rich young leader who approached Jesus to ask him what he had to do to ensure he'd go to heaven? (If not, check out Luke 18:18-25.) And remember Jesus' response to the young man's long list of "good deeds"? He said, *No one is good except God alone.* The more you know Jesus, the more this truth is self-evident. We are good only because we stay closely attached to The Only One Who Is Good.

- -

REJECT FANTASY ISLAND JESUS

The Jesus most people believe in today looks and behaves a lot like an old TV icon from the '70s—Mr. Roarke from *Fantasy Island*. If you've never seen this cheesy relic from the disco age, Mr. Roarke was something like the ageless king of Fantasy Island. He always wore white, was older but had a youthful personality, and was almost always smooth, encouraging, and nice. But he could be stern—especially with people who were trying to trick him or who had bad motives. *He existed to make the dreams of good people come true.* You couldn't really know him—watching the show you never learn anything about his private life or what drives him. He was powerful but distant. If you stayed on his good side, things were OK. He is an accurate stand-in for the Jesus we think we know, but don't. Mr. Roarke is not Jesus. Thank God.

REJECT TROJAN HORSE JESUS

For more than 20 years I've written a column for Group Magazine called Youth Ministry Minute. After all those columns, the piece I titled "The Trojan Horse" remains the most talked-about. The point of the column was to expose a false belief embedded in a lot of popular Christian music. Most people know that a Trojan horse is a metaphor for an enemy that looks very much like a friend. It's from a story in Homer's *Iliad*, where the Greeks offer their sworn foes, the Trojans, a giant wooden horse, ostensibly as a peace offering. But after the unsuspecting Trojans drag the horse inside their city walls, Greek soldiers drop out of the horse's hollow belly and open the city gates to their army, which rushes through the gates and captures Troy.

The Trojan horse I found in a lot of Christian music is the false expectation that Jesus exists to do our bidding—that he's a sort of butler we've hired to give us what we want, when we want it. And when we don't need our butler, we'd prefer that he stay out of sight in the back of the house. We'll never know Jesus better as long as we treat him as if he were our butler.

REJECT LAZY THINKING

Lazy thinking says, "We hold these truths to be self-evident." Jesus-centered thinking says, "We hold no truths as self-evident except for those that have been revealed by Jesus." So, we engage the many "truths" that pelt us in everyday life with some hard-working questions:

- Is it true within the boundaries of things Jesus actually said and did?

- Is it true based on what I already know is true about Jesus and the kingdom of God?

- Is it the full truth, or does it represent only disconnected snippets of truth?

- Is it a culturally bent truth that serves a self-centered agenda?

REJECT RELIGION MASQUERADING AS CHRISTIANITY

A youth pastor friend told me this story: "I spent some time this year leading a mission trip overseas—something happened inside of me during that time. When I came back, I told my kids, 'I'm sick of being a Christian—I'm ready to become a Christ-follower.' For the kids in my church, there's nothing I've ever said that resonated more with them, or longer. These are kids who've grown up in the church, and they want more." You'll know you're ready for a bigger helping of Jesus in your life when you, like my friend, can honestly say, "I'm sick of being a Christian—I'm ready to be a Christ-follower."

REJECT TRANSACTIONAL GRAVITY

It sounds way too dramatic, but I believe "Who do I say that Jesus is?" is pretty much the *only question* we really need for growing in our relationship with him. It's a perfect replacement for the more transactional question most of are asking instead: "What can Jesus do for me?" When you're less concerned about getting stuff from Jesus and you're more interested in knowing him better, you find yourself worshipping him one way or another almost all the time.

REJECT SHORTCUTS

Do we live our lives looking for shortcuts? I know I often have. If there's a shorter distance between two points—whether I'm running errands in my car or reading my Bible or helping out a friend—I'm tempted to take it. But when the great poet Robert Frost wrote, "Two roads diverged in a wood, and I—I took the one less traveled by," he was describing a way of life that honors the long way over the shortcut. The (false) shortcut to a life of meaning and purpose is a path called "Use God to Get What I Want in Life"—the "road less traveled" is called "the Way, the Truth, and Life." He also goes by the name of Jesus, and one of the chief practitioners of shortcut living in history, a "Pharisee of Pharisees" named Saul (later known as Paul), said this about him: *More than that, I count all things to be loss in view of the surpassing value of knowing Christ Jesus my Lord, for whom I have suffered the loss of all things, and count them but rubbish so that I may gain Christ (Philippians 3:8).*

REJECT THE CARDIGAN JESUS

I was talking with a junior high girl who'd just served as a leader in a church-wide worship experience during Holy Week. She was giddy with excitement about the whole thing. I told her I'd been asking teenagers to describe Jesus to me…just because I was curious. She thought a bit, and then said: "Well, I'd have to say he's really, really nice."

I waited for more, but there was no more. So I asked, "Remember that time Jesus made a whip and chased all the moneychangers out of the temple? Does that story change the way you describe Jesus?" She thought and thought and thought. Finally, with the tone of someone raising a white flag over a crumbling wall, she said, "Well, I know Jesus is nice, so what he did must have been nice."

I nodded and smiled grimly. She was describing that "Mister Rogers" Jesus we've already unmasked. In Matthew 23 Jesus tells the Pharisees they are "hopeless"—not once, but *seven times* in a row—and then he put the cherry on the top of that poisonous sundae by calling them "manicured grave plots," "total frauds," and "snakes." Not so nice. And that's good, because a *merely* nice Jesus is no Jesus at all—he's like a declawed version of Narnia's Aslan. And a declawed Jesus is not strong and fierce and big enough to walk with us into the fiery furnace of our everyday lives.

THE BEAUTIFUL DECLARATIONS

A few ridiculously inspirational everyday assertions

I WILL LET COURAGE RULE MY OTHER VIRTUES!

"Be strong and courageous!" When God placed the mantle of leadership on Joshua after Moses' death, he charged him to be "strong and courageous" three times in four verses (Joshua 1:6-9). I was reminded of the primacy of courage when I watched *The Late Show With David Letterman* a day or two after the 9/11 attacks and he said this: "There's only one requirement of any of us, and that is to be courageous. Because courage, as you might know, defines all other human behavior. And, I believe—because I've done a little of this myself—pretending to be courageous is just as good as the real thing."[18] It takes courage to follow Jesus. This is why he said this, in John 16:33 (NIV): *"In this world you will have trouble. But take heart! I have overcome the world."* In this context, "take heart" means the same thing as "Be strong and courageous!" To live in the spirit of Jesus is to live under the influence of courage. Take your heart with you into the dangerous twists and turns of your life today.

I WILL MAKE TRUTH MY CONQUEST!

I meet with Doug Ashley, a Denver youth pastor, once a month for lunch. Not long ago, as we were gathering our stuff to leave, our waitress stopped, got very serious, then advised us to "Be safe!" As she left, I gave Doug a "What was that?" look and then said, "That's a strange way to say goodbye." Of course, "Be safe!" isn't a strange goodbye for a lot of people today—more and more of us use it as our default substitute for "See ya." It sounds vaguely caring and savvy, but since when did "Be safe!" become our best advice? When safety becomes our filter and our passion and our best advice, we've turned from our allegiance to God's kingdom and pledged fidelity to the kingdom of this world. Jesus didn't urge his followers to "Be safe!" But he did say things like this:

- "Do not be afraid" (Luke 5:10).

- "Go in peace" (Luke 8:48).

- "Proclaim the kingdom of God!" (Luke 9:60).

- "Go and do what I do" (Luke 10:37).

- "Be awake and alert!" (Luke 21:36).

Jesus is called "the Way, the Truth, and the Life"—to live closely to Jesus is to love the truth, because the Bible also tells us that the truth sets us free. That's just another way of saying that Jesus sets us free. But in any case, try this little experiment, even for just one hour of one day—just to see what happens in you and in others. Whenever you say goodbye to someone, simply substitute "Be true!" for whatever you usually say. After your experiment, notice what has changed in you. You'll have more of Jesus, I'm thinking.

74

I WILL LIVE LARGE!

My friend Bob Krulish loves to encourage the "wheat" in my heart, so he'll often punctuate our conversations with his favorite exhortation: "Live large." When he does this, Bob is reminding me to live my life to the full extent of who I am and what God has called me to do. Living small means to live disconnected from our true nature and calling— living large means to agree with Jesus about our place in his great rescue operation. Today, did you live large or did you live small? If you're like me, you probably "lived medium." But tomorrow is another day— another chance to truly live large for Jesus.

I WILL BE CHRIST'S!

I remember an old story that J. Sidlow Baxter, a legendary English pastor and author, used to tell about a retired Scottish pastor he often passed on the lane near his home. Baxter once asked the old man, "How are you keeping?" The man responded, "I'm not keeping, I'm kept." Of all the things we can "be," nothing beats "Christ's." Not long ago I was struggling with a hard thing that had happened to me—I was having a pretty heated conversation with God about it, wrestling with some hard things about myself. At one point I cried out: "God, who am I, really?" And in the stillness that followed, I "heard" him say to me this short reply, which set me free: "Rick, the only thing you are is mine." Now, many, many times a day, I silently remind myself of this truth: "The only thing I am is his." Pick a day, any day, and try doing the same thing. At the end of the day ask yourself what has changed in you, if anything.

I WILL LIVE DANGEROUSLY!

In John 14 Jesus tells his disciples a staggering truth: *"The person who trusts me will not only do what I'm doing but even greater things"*

(John 14:12 The Message). Are we expecting to do greater things than Jesus? *Wild at Heart* author John Eldredge once told me that Christian adults have erred when we've told teenagers that your highest calling is to be nice when we should be telling you to be dangerous-for-Jesus instead. Amen. What does it mean for you to live dangerously-for-Jesus today? Most likely, it means that you're taking risks on behalf of your relationship with Jesus. Pause for a moment and ask him this simple question: "How can I do something dangerous for you today?" Wait until you sense a "something to do" or a "something to be," and then act on it.

I WILL KEEP IT IN THE LIGHT!

Nothing neutralizes our impact for God's kingdom faster, broader, and deeper than living in the shadows. Whatever we do, we must focus on living in the light—whatever we think we need to hide about ourselves we, instead, drag it out of the shadows and into the light, where others can see it. The more we do this, the more we feel free from the cords that have tied us up and imprisoned us. Jesus is not afraid of Satan, because he has nothing to hide: *"He has nothing in Me"* (John 14:30). The more you drag things into the light in your life, the less leverage your enemy has in your life and the more you'll feel free to bring good impact into the lives of others.

I WILL STAY AWAKE!

I think much of our culture is living life asleep at the wheel—that's one reason why we see so many roadside wrecks in families today. Jesus told us to stay alert because there's a "roaring lion" stalking us—and he wasn't kidding. What do you do to stay awake when you're tired and can't afford to be tired? Is it coffee? Red Bull®? Willpower? Whatever you do, I wonder if you'd consider adopting a similar strategy to stay awake to Jesus, and to the schemes of the "roaring lion" in your life. Take one minute every day, no matter what time of the day works best for you, to read 60 seconds of "the red stuff" in your Bible. The "red stuff" is the red type that a lot of Bible translations use to signify Jesus' words. Every day, spend one minute reading something Jesus said. Then kick it around in your head through the day.

I WILL ARMOR UP!

The Apostle Paul's parting advice for everyday living, offered to the Christians living in the pagan city of Ephesus, was this: *Therefore, take up the full armor of God, so that you will be able to resist in the evil day, and having done everything, to stand firm (Ephesians 6:13)*. Once you accept Jesus' warning—that there's a "roaring lion" stalking you—it only makes sense that you'd put on the armor he's offering you as protection against harm. So, he tells us to "gird our loins with truth" and "put on the breastplate of righteousness" and "shod our feet with the preparation of the gospel of peace" and "take up the shield of faith" and "the helmet of salvation" and "the sword of the spirit, which is the word of God." Wow, that's a lot of armor to put on every day. Instead of working hard to figure out what all this means for you, why not do something simpler? Today, and every day, ask Jesus to simply "dress you" before you leave your bedroom for the day. Jesus said, "You have not because you ask not." So take him at his word and ask.

80

I WILL BOOST MY NUMBER!

A friend in youth ministry once told me his system for translating an honest commitment into action. For example, because you're reading this book, you're probably open to growing in your relationship with Jesus or reading your Bible more often or even praying more often. So ask yourself: "On a scale of 1 to 10—with 1 representing 'Not' and 10 representing 'For Sure'—how doable is this goal in my life?" Once you've determined where you are on that scale, ask yourself what it will take to move you from that number to one higher. What little baby step can you take, right now, to move you one number closer to 10?

THE ORBITAL QUESTIONS

A question-a-month to chew on, over and over, in your pursuit of Jesus (plus a collection of holiday-themed questions)

THE JANUARY QUESTION

Which word comes closest to describing the way you see Jesus: *nice*, *fierce*, or *mysterious*? Explain. (Read Revelation 5:5.) Today, what word would you use to describe Jesus? Why?

THE FEBRUARY QUESTION

Jesus plainly said, *"I am the way, and the truth, and the life; no one comes to the Father, but through Me"*—so why do we so often believe that "being a good person" is how we get to heaven? (Read John 14:6.) Today, how has Jesus been your way, truth, or life?

THE MARCH QUESTION

Jesus said, *"I am the vine, you are the branches…for apart from Me you can do nothing"*—what did he really mean when he used the word *nothing*? (Read John 15:5.) What's one way you have depended on Jesus today?

THE APRIL QUESTION

After Jesus made his "you must eat my flesh and drink my blood" statement on a hillside to thousands of his "followers," all but a handful of them left in a big huff—they were disgusted by what he'd said. So Jesus asked his disciples, *"You do not want to leave too, do you?"* (Read John 6:53-67.) Assume Jesus is asking you, right now, the very same question. Today, how would you answer Jesus' question, and why?

THE MAY QUESTION

Let's say your phone rings today and it's Jesus calling—he wants to take you to dinner at your favorite restaurant tonight. Today, what's the *one thing* you'd want Jesus to know about you as you sit down to dinner with him? (Read Luke 19:1-5.)

THE JUNE QUESTION

What's the difference, if any, between loving Jesus for who he is and loving him for what he can do? (Read John 6:25-59.) Today, what's one unique thing about Jesus that causes you to feel grateful?

THE JULY QUESTION

Jesus once told a story about an employee who was about to get fired because he was lazy, lying, and a cheater. So the man secretly met with all his boss's creditors and cut what they owed in half so that, after he was fired, he'd get some help from them. At the end of the story Jesus praised the man's shrewdness and said God's people are not very shrewd. What does it mean to be shrewd, and why are we typically bad at it? (Read Luke 16:1-9.) Today, what's one opportunity you have to be "good and shrewd" on behalf of Jesus?

THE AUGUST QUESTION

Every day reread the story Jesus told called the parable of the prodigal son (Luke 15:11-32), then ask: What is Jesus trying to say about God's character and personality?

THE SEPTEMBER QUESTION

All of us were taught to not call other people hurtful names, but Jesus called the Pharisees "snakes," "whitewashed tombs," and "hypocrites"— how do you explain what Jesus did? (Read Matthew 23:1-33.) Today, look for one way to honor the spirit of Jesus and "speak truth to power."

THE OCTOBER QUESTION

Jesus spent a good deal of his ministry time identifying and casting out demons—why doesn't this happen more often in our lives today? (Read

Matthew 8:28-34.) In what ways, if any, are you "casting out demons" in your sphere of influence?

THE NOVEMBER QUESTION

Jesus seemed to like hanging out with the fringe people of his day—prostitutes, tax collectors, the sick and maimed. What drew Jesus to these people? (Read Matthew 21:31-32.) Today, how are you like one of the "fringe people"? Today, how can you live in the spirit of Jesus and do something kind for a "fringe person"?

THE DECEMBER QUESTION

If you sat down next to Jesus on an airplane (of course he'd switch seats to give you the window), what are the first three questions you think he'd ask you (besides your name)? (Read Luke 9:18-20.) Today, what's one question you'd like Jesus to ask you?

THE NEW YEAR'S DAY QUESTION

Most good friendships are based on mutual giving—it's pretty easy to understand what Jesus can offer us, but what do we have to offer Jesus that he doesn't already have? (Read John 15:14-15.)

THE VALENTINE'S DAY QUESTION

Jesus never married, and we have no indication he was ever romantically interested in anyone—but do you think he ever flirted with a girl? Why or why not? (Read Matthew 22:24-30.)

THE EASTER QUESTION

Sometimes people who don't believe in Jesus say the biblical accounts about him were made up by the Bible's authors. What's something Jesus said or did that makes you think no one could have made it up?

THE INDEPENDENCE DAY QUESTION

Jesus often withdrew by himself to spend time alone—why do you think he needed so much alone time? (Read Luke 5:16.)

THE HALLOWEEN QUESTION

If Jesus was a little boy during our time, would he go trick-or-treating at Halloween? Why or why not? If you think he would, what costume would he wear? (Read Matthew 4:10.)

THE THANKSGIVING QUESTION

Jesus said he was going to prepare a special room in his "Father's house" for each of us—what do you think your room will look like? What do you hope it has in it? Why would Jesus put those things in your room? (Read John 14:2.)

THE ADVENT QUESTION

If Jesus were a little boy during our time, would his parents take him to see Santa? If not, why not? If so, what would Jesus ask Santa for? Explain. (Read Luke 2:22-35.)

ENDNOTES

1. N. T. Wright, *Following Jesus: Biblical Reflections on Discipleship* (Grand Rapids, MI: Eerdmans, 1994), p. ix.

2. Taken from Sermon 242, *Christ Precious To Believers*, preached by Charles Spurgeon on March 13, 1859.

3. From a description of the "mental model" theory first developed by Kenneth Craik for his book *The Nature of Explanation* (1943), now out of print.

4. From a description of the story of Richard Jewell at wikipedia.org.

5. Donald Miller, *Searching for God Knows What* (Nashville, TN: Thomas Nelson, 2004), 157-159.

6. From a story by Henri Nouwen in his book *The Road to Daybreak*, Reissue Edition (New York, NY: Image Books, 1990).

7. Mark Galli, *Jesus Mean and Wild: The Unexpected Love of an Untamable God* (Grand Rapids, MI: Baker Books, 2006), 112.

8. From a presentation by Dr. David Walsh to the Cherry Creek School District's "Parent Information Network" meeting in Denver, Colorado, on October 3, 2006.

9. Insights from *Prayer: Does It Make Any Difference?* by Philip Yancey (Grand Rapids, MI: Zondervan, 2006).

10. Taken from *Now Discover Your Strengths* by Marcus Buckingham and Donald Clifton (New York, NY: Free Press, 2001).

11. From "Lovers in a Dangerous Time," written and recorded by Bruce Cockburn on the album *Stealing Fire* (1984).

12. Ned Erickson learned this progression from his ministry partners in Young Life.

13. From Steve Merritt's "Personal Growth" column in the November/December 2006 issue of Group Magazine.

14. From a brief biographical paper, "The Story of Ignaz Philipp Semmelweis" by William C. Wood, M.D.

15. Eugene Peterson, from the foreword for *Jesus Mean and Wild: The Unexpected Love of an Untamable God* by Mark Galli (Grand Rapids, MI: Baker Books), 11.

16. Christian Smith and Melinda Lundquist Denton, *Soul Searching: The Religious and Spiritual Lives of American Teenagers* (New York, NY: Oxford University Press, 2005).

17. From a sidebar titled "Whose Life Is It Anyway?" by Tim McTague, in the July 2006 issue of CCM Magazine.

18. From David Letterman's biography on the website imdb.com.